Radical Dances of the Ferocious Kind

Radical Dances of the Ferocious Kind

Poems

Tina Tru

atmosphere press

Contents

for family of origin and chosen fam — revolutionary love to all

/

"All poets, all writers are political.
They either maintain the status quo, or they say,
'Something's wrong, let's change it for the better.'"

~ Sonia Sanchez

PROLOGUE

Yesterday I watched a video with Naomi Klein called "Coronavirus Capitalism – and How to Beat It." In it, Klein connects the concept of disaster capitalism from her book *Shock Doctrine* and the COVID-19 crisis as capitalism's perfect disaster. I glance at pictures of graffiti from New York: "Capitalism is the Virus."

The meaning of apocalypse: to "unveil" or "uncover," informs my role as a poet: to tell the truth. I wake up livid, often shouting the words of Che Guevara: "It's not my fault if reality is Marxist!" and marching to the kitchen for instant coffee. This moment we are in seems apocalyptic, or at least, a world reminiscent of multi-media series on loop: Black Mirror meets Blade Runner meets Parable of the Sower.

Alice Walker wrote, "Poetry is the lifeblood of revolution, rebellion and raising consciousness." My hope is that poetry continues to bridge us across a "if I cannot dance it's not my revolution" (Emma Goldman), better world we know is possible.

From *Freedom is a Constant Struggle*:

> *"I don't think we have any alternative other than remaining optimistic. Optimism is an absolute necessity, even if it's only optimism of the will, as Gramsci said, and pessimism of the intellect. What has kept me going has been the development of new modes of community. I don't know whether I would have survived had not movements survived, had not communities of resistance, communities of struggle. It is in collectives that we find reservoirs of hope and optimism... We cannot be moderate. We will have to be willing to stand up and say no with our combined spirits, our collective intellects, and many bodies."*

Angela Davis' words highlight the importance of the personal as political and the political as social. Karl Marx knew that: our consciousness comes from being social beings. This is difficult in isolation, but doable with accessible technology.

I viewed the same Naomi Klein video today via Zoom (as we are in quarantine) with comrades from the Winston-Salem Democratic Socialists of America. I remember joining my first socialist group (the International Socialist Organization) after reading *This Changes Everything: Capitalism versus the Climate.*

Her call for "the power of ferocious love" to combat racism, sexism, climate change and capitalism made me think of dance. In these distressing times, I invite y'all to explore, organize, and dance with *Radical Dances of the Ferocious Kind.*

FREE HEALTHCARE
Free testing, treatment and healthcare for all.

NO WORK
Suspend work obligations. Guarantee food stamps and sick pay for all.

NO PAYING — NO DEBT
Suspend all rent, mortgage, utilities, loans, foreclosures, evictions and parking enforcement.

FREE THE PRISONERS
End bail for jails, deactivate ICE, release detainees, and stop all sweeps of homeless camps.

HOMES FOR ALL
Open up unoccupied homes to anyone who needs one.

@ash_antifa

RADICAL DANCES OF THE FEROCIOUS KIND

Revolutionary love is a radical dance of the ferocious kind.
Beyond denotation and connotation

Morning stretches and jellyrolls
Más allá de their mermaid.

A cackle
Between a card catalog and meme.
Ella singing La India
A lavender bud
on my forehead.

Coffee covered soccer talks
Between two old babies.

It's probably beyond the spiraling
of fall leaves and
Better than the transition of bread
to toast;
Or the stillness of chamomile tea after carnival.

Quizás es como Digable Planets and *Ana Tijoux,*
That sparks the movement of two (or more)
hydrangeas: purple, green and blue.

Certainly, it's the continued imagining,
practicing,
studying,
trying
a dance with red heart(s)
as radical and ferocious as you.

Richmond Strike of May 6, 1937

Miss Louise 'Mamma' Harris
Long, gray hair pulled back in a bun
Wore a stern smile, never a dress.
As she listened to Bennie's son.
Yes, she talked with Bennie's son.

"For more than five decades," he did say,
"almost 83 hours a week
my father stemmed tobacco every day
for a measly 20 cents with 18.
For a measly 20 cents with 18.

"You'd only get paid for the stems!"
he cried to Miss Mamma Louise.
Stoic she turned to him in reply:
"No, we never got paid for the leaf."
"No, we never got paid for the leaf".

Until one warm spring day, fed up with it
As Miss Louise continued to speak:
"Your father got tired of being paid stems
For measly 20 cents with 18.
A measly 20 cents with 18.

Mamma continued, "We gave them hell.
400 of us women and 20 males.
And he, the picket-captain!" She stood tall
As she told him this great tale.
Yes, she told him this great tale.

But the cops were on us without avail
"And he was hit across the head
The blow was hard, it took him out"

Know this, son: "Your father was brave
And us women, do not forget.
And with action of Jackson and of Aston
We did what was needed in the fight.

Daylight after the L.A. Rebellion

It's not stealing if you're in need.
Say them without a contact and
a dancer with a headache.
Whatever you need honey
she remembers the white man in the suit
telling both of them.

What once was a butting black-eyed Susan wedged
In between a gray concrete parking slab
and a brick wall of the club
is dead.

What is spring in LA anyway?

A disheveled palm tree covered in
urine pushes the workers
to the side of the empty parking lot.
sun shines
exposing scars, raw teeth
and fatigue.

TATA'S HOUSE

Uncle John shows me soccer with my left foot.

(My family still wonders why I'm a socialist.)

They're sunny days at Peck Park, mostly afternoons

post-Catholic school.

We slurp banana milkshakes

and on Fridays, churros con chocolate

(the stout, short kind with dense lava).

We swing from the walnut tree on W. 13th St.

The passageway of the colonial breeds a cloud of butterflies,

anchored by stucco that permeates velvet laundry soap,

gofres, and manifestos from Las Ramblas.

Yellow succulents of the Spanish Civil War and San Pedro
palms

create a particular type of heaven -- a Woolfian uncertainty

where I am capable of managing doubt.

I remember Rebecca Solnit on Gonzalez:

"Despair is a confident memory of the future."

I remember Peter, Paul and Mary. And old Alanis.

The Sea Inside: On the Origin of Love

Sand fill(ament)s one hundred milliseconds,
love lounges in the limbic system;
a dynamic support of turquoise subconscious
reveals motivation reef and SOFAR channel.
Marshmallow tests were wrong; we don't live
in past shores, with a third of a second delay
on the wave break.
The knowledge of neuroplasticity means
hope in love.

It does, however, manifest with four-minute stares into
windows,
and analysis of three thousand facial expressions.
It's now a cocaine addiction: Every. where. ness.
Add language exchange turned Scrabble competition.
(Lovesex: voxes, exes, voxel.)
Then there's the change: us, social beings.
Hurston knew:
"Love is like the sea. It's a moving thing."
Repeat with an attempt on a new coastline.

Time: A Thing

"You do not pack a gun unless you're prepared to use it."
- Clifford Simack, *Time is the Simplest Thing*

To combat green light envy: 1. Realize yellow's fine in the South, and
2. Bubble universes offer an alternative: eternal inflation.
I feign fights and coordinate sensimilla flights,
but find laments in the freezer: *eats ice and suspects anemia*
the crunch relieves rejection and love's lost (nursing) lounge.

In the 5th dimension crystal palace, I danced salsa in Fibonacci:
down the stairway Familia Sagrada within a cloud of butterflies.
At Sunrise Acres, the gait belt is too loose for Harold, 92;
My body, between glass plates, is in triangle pose; and
to refrain from sternocleidomastoid strain: I breathe.

Does the lily pad of breath and busy sustain life?
I work on my story - a Southern drama starring westerners
(from different subfields) and a packing nurse, who
instead of wrapping up a routine dressing change,
pours alcohol over the wound and ignores his call bell.

THE LOOTING

We walk in front of the museum. Who decided the
compensations of humanity? An illicit
trade here, illuminated by a dark lantern old furnishings
and
the bustle of young men.
This is a story of the biggest blow in a face
that hadn't drawn blood.
They erased the Humanity's
Footprints.
.History vanished in the dark.
The unlit basement had been unable to find
them again.
What had been taken (or "missing") we know were 4,795 cylinder
seals, 5,542 coins, glass bottles, beads, amulets, and jewelry;
The Treasure of Nimrud, 1,000 pieces of gold, crowns,
necklaces, rosettes, bracelets and precious stones from the
eighth century BC.
The Sacred Vase of Warka dated from 3200
B.C., the Mask of Warka the Golden Harp of Ur, the
Bassetki Statue and the twin copper Ninhursag Bulls-
Gone forever.
Confusion.
Frames fallen. Naked walls.
Above the center door to the main building is a large handwritten
sign: 'Death to all Americans and Zionist pigs'.
A Sunni archeologist felt authorized to speak:
"We had cried for help several times!"
We who have been forgotten.
History thrown away by Amerikkka
The details are found in a Texas Instrument of public education.
Now you know the US invasion killed
the cradle of humanity.

Friday Mountain Fire in North Carolina

"What of Terra, the ancient earth?"
- Ursula Le Guin *The Dispossessed*

Contents include: carbon dioxide
methane
nitrous oxide
photo chemically reactive compounds:
carbon monoxide (CO),
nonmethane volatile organic carbon (NMVOC),
nitrogen oxides (NOx),
and coarse particulate matter (PM)
a convective plume integration
of emissions

I smell cinnamon prisms
on corners of my glasses
red-orange sky flashbacks of
a brushfire calamity

AFTER YOU

The center of this galaxy
smells like rum and raspberries.
Indeed, two objects will eventually meet without gravity,
Around a fluid wall of sound where mind is love and time,
Inside: a radical dance of riot unicorns and summer vines.
Desire nestled in this book.
Intersect with you and - look -

Your eyes hold many colors
of sea water, of youth
You grab my arm to confirm my colorless tattoo
Lean in to kiss me
sex and gaiety
texts and a movie

A Spanish jazz song
Nunca será lo mismo
knows my loss, too
It will never be the same
after you

Y-12 Break In

It's 2 o'clock in the morning and all the equipment is ready to be placed in the white van. They don't have far to travel - just one mile up a dirt road past the post office, and a slight right back Albert Road. Terry, a thin medium-height bearded man places the large ladder in the trunk while Sister Rosa puts a bag of items (three LED flashlights, some wire cutters, walkie talkies, a pager, and an extra hoodie) in the black of the van. Jack is reviewing the plan, pen in mouth as he scratches the small curls of hair left on his head. Jack is the Vietnam Vet, interested in logistics and strategy. What is the best way to climb atop the facility? He doubted his own strategy. Terry, finished with ladder, gave him a gentle pat on the back, " Don't worry Jack", he reassured him as if he read his mind. "This is the most effective and efficient way to do this. We are ready." Sister Rosa held her rosary and said a silent prayer sitting on the edge of the opened trunk. It was the Serenity Prayer: "God grant me the serenity to accept the things I cannot change, the courage to change the things I can and the wisdom to know the difference." Seemed like an odd prayer for this type of occasion. Terry overheard Rosa and chimed in, " I know that prayer from AA." Sister Rosa smiled. "Ready to rock and roll," she said. They gathered together and held hands to form a small circle " We are stewards of this Earth. We are the guardians of this one planet doing something we must do for the future, for our children." Terry teared up as it was time to go. An 83-year-old nun, a Vietnam vet, and a house painter were about to break into the largest nuclear facility in the United States.

Drone Day

Today I saw a drone on 4th,

wedged between the Nissan and
Mellow Mushroom pizza.

It circled pie, flashed tomato red.

A girl shouted. A leaf screamed.

We shall shake this small southern town.

We can shake this, slow but steady.

What's it like drunk driving on 40?
What's it like dodging honesty?

Who knows what is a church home?

Only the drone.

All the Fairies of the Last Forest

"Did you ever wonder if you liked long hot showers because they washed away your sins Or did you like the way no Gender could exist inside of a fogged-up mirror?"–Kimmy Rae Fisher

Coffee grounds expand the cotton candy hydrangeas. Live oaks line the Last Forest. Prism membranes reflect the multi-universes within and with(out) in semi-permeable shells. There are more Masoquistas than Owlous; but each dimension is represented in fairy form: Ferns, Robins, Carbonites, Tonis, Bobs, Wolfbirds, Firecats, Stonemilkers and Reefkids. Every fairy has three names, and some have four or five. K-roaches seek to destroy all the dimensions of consciousness through the destruction of fingers. In response, all the fairies peel off the digit tips of each other. Lulunas are kept in mauve boxes and buried. The remaining parts of the tips are used as gas for defense. On solstice, two Stonemilkers were approached by a roach to change affiliation, but the fairies were persuaded by the solidarity compact of varied permutation. This community consciousness inspires even the saddest Masoquista to choose love over pain. In the fog of the Last Forest, the red-orange moon glowed like a circus rose.

On the penultimate day of Leo rising, roaches called Parasites, had invaded a Toni's treehouse. These roaches were under a special group – PUKE: Parasites Under K-roach Enterprise -- and targeted undocumented fairies. As a response, the fairies formed PUKE watches to protect Tonis and other fairies. This time, in Terrabilly, the neighboring fairies formed a circle chain around the treehouse and ensured that the Toni remained safe in their treehouse. The recent raids by PUKE have sparked intense fear among many communities of fairies - but the fairies persist and resist to save themselves and their home, the Last Forest.

JELLYFISH

Turritopsis dohrnii is
the Benjamin Button
of bacterial gelatinous domes.
The key to immortality –
they clone themselves.
"Medusa rejuvenate!"
The pink meanie consumes
thirty-four of itself.
Some look like plastic bags.
Most will eat peanut butter.
Peanut butter jellyfish.
Peanut butter jellyfish.

ONE REAL SPIN

disco prodding
bachata spins
rumba biscuits
until the end

march on, woman
resist, man
make me care
salient friend

late night texts
but not too late
are you coupled?
what's your take?

roots sink in
as ant line turns
a parade of raisins
captures the fern

a clock melts wall
jalapeño cat prance
jealous blue-green
waiting to dance

no health, no time
to deconstruct it
move on forward
sans your loveship

yes, this wolf woman
demands respect
your quiet betrayal
do you regret?

whatever, we'll see
an oak tree unites
in Gernika, waits
a sweet Basque flight

Bottom Up Bloom

Bottom up beauty. A collective of
Multi-faceted *flores* in working hands.
The soil couldn't grow ego
Nor create gatekeepers. So
How did our bouquet emerge?
Brown spiral roots of underground.
Black base. Proletariat pebbles.
Some hard, semi, and soft.
Movement of earth: water, sun, time.
Synthesizing structural growth
Of radical roots manifest
Every working part. The roles:
1.Unique pedals move with wind.
2. Stamen needs anther to produce
pollen. 3. Filament supports the anther.
4. Ovule is central. A pistol.
Because we flourish
from different stems
It's no inflorescence.
We are held in bunch, an essence
of synaptic struggles connecting
daily development.
All the Little gems.
Red tulips.
Wildflowers.
Pansies.
Lastly: we don't blame
depression on the flower, no. Instead we grow
new soil Together.

Children of Peace

junior reserve officers' training corps
J ROT C
Juniors rot c? Juniors rot you see
when he perfects how to gun
U.S.-isms –
racism
exceptionalism
capitalism
militarism
imperialism
sexism
Root Systems of us
Who are we if we're not
A base in Kuwait?
The detention desert
in Baja California?
Our county jail up the street?
A Palestinian child
stares us in the face
shakes their head:
"Another killer from the States."

Everything My Love Is

my love's a hot superconductor,
metastable like metallic hydrogen,
this means at high temperature, you
release him, and he stays the same pressure.

we combine energy to build a train:
magnetic levitation for the masses,
a platinum bullet, that transports
all to an ambiguous utopia.

my love's the blue ridge mountains,
every charnockite suite. Grateful Riff:
"I've been all around this world,"
yet, *hoy*, we share similar coordinates.

in an unknown palm, our curves touch,
we're a crew of cloudberries, picked and
carried to Cannon Beach. we brighten
this gray backdrop with our sunshine fire.

my love's the best hot dog stand
(with a vast selection of chips).
he's BUSY. all. night. long. always local,
but never centrally located.

together we're hot dog and stand,
proletariat power and sustenance.
fuck bougie eats. fuck bougie eats.
we're on wheels and we can move.

my love's a Mola masterpiece,
by the Kuna Indians of Colombia.
dark foundation with bright stitches
of nature from the Global South.

from Colón to Cartagena,
I absorb the dresses, people,
city, plants and sea:
everything my love is.

my love's the succulent garden
on the corner of Cherry and 2nd.
orange, green, purple: weathers
California heat: wild, calm, eco.

this garden connects with mine
but I contain cacti and prickly pear,
I am sustainable, but
not as smooth as my love.

my love is some kind of Spain
where the barrel curves left.
his stare invades like the surf
of a vulnerable soapwash.

I, too, am the famous wave.
the outer lip, to be exact
but my windows are opaque,
and in the tide, I look away.

my love's a South Pole glacier,
with a shield volcano as his layer.
a steady accumulation of lava sheets,
creates his warrior shield.

LET US

Let's promote open humble socialism.
Meet me between opportunist hacktivism
and ideological purity.
It's not mutually exclusive, see?
Today: Bi-visibility –
Use heart, courage and brain.
Two Dance to the Wizard of Oz again.

Grow Your Own Brain/
Spacetime Entanglement

building tissues in a culture is not new.
step 1: add nutrients to tiny balls of cells
step 2: wait and isolate
step 3: add proteins
and voila! You have an organoid like a mouse or rat
though rats, we know, do the right thing –
even if there is no treat.
the highly folded human brain
overcomplicates everything.

In 1939 it was discovered that various cells
in a frog embryo will seek each
other out and regenerate their shape

what happens when minds separate
and seek out in space?

One could, for example, entangle particles of a certain kind—

     Mr. Blue, Ms. Glee

at one location with particles of a different find—

       the sea

at the same location
 essential worker two,
and you, also matter.

Maybe a universe separates
And a multiverse reunites.

NEW ROTATION

A sepia roulette wheel
is Foucault's un-reality.
Everyone loses friends
during a new rotation.

Distance and silence
turns woman into wolf. I run
on days I need you,
all mornings without sun.

The sensual form
is a brain and heart attack,
but, when survived,
Dance grows a mauve-green lettuce patch.

This *paz* dispenser speaks:
"One pill makes you calm."
My brain, in 5th Dimension,
has the *Wedding Bell Blues.*

Charlottesville, USA

We stopped at a Bojangles on the way.
                      Crossing state lines
with Black Star and strategy
        to Charlottesville, USA.

At the center park.
Hurry up and wait.
Hurry up and wait.
Gather, chatter.
August 12, 2017.

The white supremacists
across the streets
circled us with flags and polos.
No tiki torches this time.

A group of comrades
walked counter-round on the nearby
sidewalk.

I remember a bandana, a queer buzz cut,
velvet
like microvilli and a sense of calm
surprised me.
Who keeps us safe?

At one point we were trapped in a tunnel. No
movement.
Another time, we were quiet. Respect for
neighbors.
Then we were loud: "Antifascista"

The crash came too fast to react. I saw a
comrade
with blood on her hands. I hugged two
people.
Breathed with many.
Who keeps us safe?

The Dandelion May Have Lost My Smile

The dandelion may have lost my smile.
My smile surfs the Arctic
to Mediterranean shores,
and barrels from North to West
to the Southern Ocean.

It scales Mt. Rainier
as a mauve leather jacket,
and hides in Hanging Rock,
in a cave unknown.

It climbs planes
near Corporate von Psychopath,
then dives to prep death for
one long, last drop at Angel Falls.

It lives in Mariana Trench,
in a dark, quiet deepness,
eats the wood of old ships,
in a cold only some know.

It floats as a cirrus cloud,
20,000 feet from Earth,
and flies to bubble universes
of eternal inflation.

It rots around my toilet ring,
as red rod serratia,
and grows (x)fold inside, only
to die at the stroke of a fake tan.

Consequence of Curiosity

For the love of Science Experiments
She just wanted to explore
(curiosity-based research)
Happen if she mixed those chemicals in a bottle.
She was in-out in the open,
Mixing that shit up.
The cap came off the bottle and a
Little smoke came out, but that's
It, nothing to get
About, you know?
Some SRO type--
Said shit about
A breach of conduct, I don't know.
But the principal defended her, you know,
The principal was like, "She's a good kid.
Never been in trouble."

Then the cops came to school and
started to ask her questions.
This is the consequence of curiosity.
Imagination eliminated
From five and replaced
With test test test
Too many rules, SRO
And a roach.

GIRL ON THE RUN

She must leave
the state to get it done.
Everything's heavy-hot
a loaded gun
protruding sack
brown backpack
color like her slim arms
those bamboo legs.
Work's a drag.
School?- a dream
in a ditch – young girl
can't catch a break
True terror when the
bible belt whips you
beats you to a pulp
black-purple circles
coffee stain rings
pain makes May,
June, July every
month the cruelest one.
Why'd she wait so long?
Sherbet sky, a payphone,
Greyhound bus moans.
Total strangers in an
intimate pose, progressive
peeps unite to squash the
status quo? Ain't got
the luxury to
think politically.
He stashed
her savings in the mighty
Mississippi
With nothing left, she's
left, on the run.

WORDS

words murmur
sing, dance and scream

and connect intersect
relate reverberate

they whistle and whine and roar.

they revolt "not one more"
and assert
"know justice, know peace"

they intrigue
saudade

and illuminate
luz

they destroy
odio
and rebuild
amor.

I consume and
release them
with the expectation
of everything
and nothing
a mi manera.

Margaret Atwood on words after
word after

is power.

Bus Blues

A Black lesbian
pulls out headphones
the station lights
her wrist tattoos
and fast food visor

Across the bench
a Lumbee woman
Reads the news
In chef garb
Hair net still on

I hear a rider yell, "how much"
And a response: "one minute"
The 96 may take off
Without this transit couple

What if we decided now
we're not going to feed you?
 it's not worth the bus blues
'Cause we won't negotiate truth

What if we connected times
And refused to work, too?
'Cause It's not worth the bus blues
And we don't negotiate truth

HOPE (PANDEMIC VERSION)

the difference between
optimism and hope
is the first bite into a tomato
sweet and sun kissed
versus a store one, rotten-dull

it is the passed down story
of a *bisabuela* advising
against doing life *a lo tonto.*
Now we must be wise with
the world maps we hold in our hands

Hope is not wishing, but rather,
the power of us marching
to live and make
a liberation of radical love and
reparations, a reality

and through shock it looks like:
feeling spring bloom
cursing with tunes
laughing on zoom

ACKNOWLEDGEMENTS

Thank you to the folks at Atmosphere Press – especially Nick Coutright and Cameron Finch - for trusting me and taking a chance on an amateur poet. I am so very grateful. A special thank you to Mara Garcia Viloria for the incredible cover. Find her at @magavitart on Instagram.

I remain forever grateful for the folks of Consciousness through Poetry, especially Michael Hall and Masika Braithwaite, its geniuses and founders. Thanks to Cristian Vasquez and Rohnda Ammouri for your friendship.

Thanks to the Greensboro Revolutionary Socialists and to comrade-family in Winston-Salem, North Carolina who remind me that another world is possible.

To family, friends, and comrades who I have not mentioned by name but remain in my heart and mind – your support and love mean the world to me – *mil gracias.*

About Atmosphere Press

Atmosphere Press is an independent, full-service publisher for excellent books in all genres and for all audiences. Learn more about what we do at atmospherepress.com.

We encourage you to check out some of Atmosphere's latest releases, which are available at Amazon.com and via order from your local bookstore:

Report from the Sea of Moisture, poetry by Stuart Jay Silverman

The Enemy of Everything, poetry by Michael Jones

Giving Up The Ghost, essays by Tina Cabrera

The Stargazers, poetry by James McKee

Southen. Gay. Teacher., nonfiction by Randy Fair

The Pretend Life, poetry by Michelle Brooks

Minnesota and Other Poems, poetry by Daniel N. Nelson

Last Dance, short stories by Nicole Zelniker

Come Kill Me!, short stories by Mackinley Greenlaw

Interviews from the Last Days, sci-fi poetry by Christina Loraine

the oneness of Reality, poetry by Brock Mehler

About the Author

Tina Tru is a radical queer Feminist-Marxist and teacher who uses nature, history, and science to convey themes of loss, love, feminism and liberation. Her writing focuses on workplace conditions, food, labor rights, femmeness and LGBTQIA rights. You can find her poetry and articles in the *Tipton Poetry*  *Journal, The Bitchin' Kitsch, The Arrival, Scalawag, Monthly Review,* and *Truthout.* Between writing breaks, she enjoys dancing, reading, cooking, and lately...zooming.

Yo solo sé que escribo, luego existo
Porque la palabra cobra vida y sentido
Ana Tijoux

"The rich are only defeated when running for their lives."

~ C.L.R James

www.ingramcontent.com/pod-product-compliance
Lightning Source LLC
Chambersburg PA
CBHW021347060726
47591CB00006B/2202